Derek Johnathon Mazzei who writes as Novera Novo was born August 1st, 1974. He can be defined in many ways male, Caucasian and heterosexual. He worships The Sun, The Moon and The Earth.

He has an interest in pursuing projects in the fine arts especially in music as a computer, software, and hardware musician, and a vocalist. He further has a keen interest in pursuing the writing of other books as well as a collection of paintings.

Derek is a film virtuoso and engrosses his time in pursuit of wealth with show business, sports, medicine, natural resources, fabric, food, and construction.

To

DEREK JOHNATHON MAZZEI

Making some money.

Novera Novo

"Defending Alive:

Coming of Mazares Dead!"

Novera Novo

DEFENDING ALIVE: COMING OF MAZARES DEAD

AUSTIN MACAULEY PUBLISHERS™

LONDON • CAMBRIDGE • NEW YORK • SHARJAH

Ordering Information
Quantity sales: Special discounts are available on quantity purchases by corporations, associations, and others. For details, contact the publisher at the address below.

Publisher's Cataloging-in-Publication data
Novo, Novera
Defending Alive: Coming of Mazares Dead

ISBN 9781641820493 (Paperback)
ISBN 9781641820486 (Hardback)
ISBN 9781645364238 (ePub e-book)

Library of Congress Control Number: 2019937082

www.austinmacauley.com/us

First Published 2023
Austin Macauley Publishers LLC
40 Wall Street, 33rd Floor, Suite 3302
New York, NY 10005
USA

mail-usa@austinmacauley.com
+1 (646) 5125767

The, Sun, Moon, and Earth

The Pyramids and The Sphinx

The Inca Empire

The United States Of America

The United States Treasury

The White House

North America

South America

Central America

The United Kingdom

Australia

Antarctica

Caligula

Alexander The Greatest

Tutankhamun

Ayar Manco

Nostradamus

Amerigo Vespucci

John Locke

Alexander Hamilton

James Wilson Marshall

James Jackson Jeffries

The Police

The Military

Beer

Whiskey

Magic Mushrooms

Ketamine

Intravenous

Austin Macauley Publishing

Broken Defense = Tormented Contemplation

Reason for Broken Defense = Telepathic Trafficking, Possession and Failure to Flush an exorcism.

Before beginning the reading of this novel, as the author, I decided to liberate you at the beginning rather than leave you in suspense until the end.

Powers that you gain by reading are as follows:

Defense Prophecy

Telepathy Prophecy

Leaving the body in luxury at the end of life

Entering and remaining in limbo, in luxury

Fortune Telling

Returning to the body in luxury

Fatal Prophecy, Psychic, Palm Reading,

Permission to involve in any activity consultation

Worshiping the Sun, Moon, and Earth

Reading, Writing, Understanding warning, Exorcism-Flush, and Illusion

Using Drugs and Alcohol

****Intravenous****

Prayer

No Suicide

Heterosexual

Dictatorship

The Spirit

DJ - Software Programmer

Athlete

Money

Natural Causes

Reward

Musician

Comedy

All The Power In My Lifeline

Chapter 1
Ambition

Before I began writing, the first order I was given while in prayer for power to write this book, was to pour a glass of homemade red wine with ice, then to study the medical use of ketamine drugs intravenously.

Understand: "War Timing" Corrupt permission to temporarily study allergies with *a drug*, to study guilt.

Or, to be studying a challenging energy without it being guilty…I have a list of drugs and food that I would have to war time study, temporarily. Red or Blue Steroids, Cocaine, Crack-Cocaine, Hydroponic Marijuana, Marijuana, Hashish, Acid, PCP, Morphine, Amphetamine, Tobacco, Tylenol, Whiskey, Ginger Ale, all Tomato Sauces, Whole Wheat, Beans, Horse Meat, Shark, Seal, Elephant Seal, Dolphin, Sea lion, Lobster, and Crab.

At 35 years of age, I've yet to be paid as a writer. As DJ Novera, I have numerous records and tours to accomplish. Always in progress, laboring on musical projects. That is true, I do have that power, in favor of working for the energies to confess to being guilty in the court of closed mouth law and The Judicial System. Born a Roman citizen, a few hours away from The United States' Detroit or

Buffalo border. In Toronto, York, United States Of America.

Quickly, I managed to believe that I was destined to control the Roman, American, United Kingdom and Antarctican Empire. Today, it's half the world, known as the Sun, Moon, Earth, and Human Beings Empire.

Or, power to control an election campaign at the age of 21. Since then, I have invested my time, my studied mind, and my energy in the Encyclopedia Study of (WARNING: Use prophetic attention: These drugs, and these drugs only) White Steroids, Malugin, Ecstasy, Ketamine, Crystal Meth, DMT, Opium, Peyote, Quaaludes, Barbiturates, Uppers, Downers, Liquid G. Intravenously, and using my nostrils and mouth. Gum weed, Menthol, and Peppermint cigarettes. Wine, Beer, Rum & Coke, Cognac, Scotch, Vodka, Sambuca. Rock'n'Roll, Dance Electronica music, DJing-Sequence Programming, Singing, Playing Guitar, Producing, Engineering, Acting, Directing, Writing, Bodybuilding, Baseball, Soccer, Football, Hockey, Formula 1, Indy, and Pace Car.

World touring, with a prayer powerful enough for other people to use, use it and survive. I was always interested in staying close to a prayer that involved innocent sincerity to survive with money. This is why I was comfortable with my power being at the head of leadership.

Lost full time interest in Italian politics, compatible with all people, abiding with all peaceful expectations, learning permitted drug use. In case of energy emergencies, such as authority regulations, rules, to be stronger, I gain strength within myself, granted through the power of work and prayer. Losing interest in Italian politics means, not interested in Italian politics as a full time commitment, laboring wisdom. Being recognized and considered King of English-Rome. I managed to become The Dictator of English-Rome and The United States Of America.

I should look to see if Nostradamus' prophecies had anything else to say about me. In the index, I found Mazares. I left the library as confident as I was when telling other psychic fortune-telling people with intuition and power, that I was to be born in Toronto, on August The First, named Derek Johnathon Mazares. In my studied mind, powerful enough to control the world as a musician. The way I do now. The wrath and heart of the United States Military. A War-Time Alien spy, studying new life, in a caucasian womb. I like to pray to and worship the Sun, the Moon and the Earth. The energy helps me think properly. If necessary, contacting the National Security Agency Heterosexually.

All the children of The World said, "Mazares, you have to stay away from men, women, children, drugs, food, and alcohol that weakens people, and yourself. Your children are crying for you to be their dad. You're not going to have us wrongly influenced so that you can experiment with flowers, men, and women you should stay away from, are you?"

"No, young one. I'm working to prevent attempts that would have had you influenced by improper drug use, with the young and learning. I should tell you, in case I ever fall short of my responsibility towards you, and people like you. If love is too far away from me to substitute. Aliens find a good productive room with me for good reasons."

13

The human being, separated at the genitals, praying hands, and the seeds of sex. Allow them, the not guilty, in the Synagogues, the Vatican, Mecca, Buddhists temples, East Indian polytheism. All do what they do.

I like the idea of moving with diesel. It's always faster for me and my travel time. Praying to and worshiping the Sun, the Moon, and the Earth, always adding worship to symbols that represent global warming. Sharing planet earth in the cosmos with Pagans, Wicca, Magic, Voodoo, Sorcery, and Witchcraft. Play with it, the idea of me having power in prayer. A relationship with the inventor of the human being, where power and immortality are granted. This is what I say, hear, and see about what it does and says when you work, for expert skills, to build an immortal life. Praying with hashish can score as less amount of points then with hydro marijuana.

Gum weed! You're a winner!!! Wasting more time as Mob with nostrils, speed, and heroin. Unless controlling: [War-Time-Study].

After the crime is committed justifiably, and the prayers have been answered and heard, life is pleasure with prayer, more answers, more explicit sex, and love wives.

For hours a day erect, I have the strength to accept corrupt intercourse with a wife, plus three other women. Rather than being regrettably committed to only one woman. When I was ready to tell her there is no permission available for Valiums, Cocaine, Crack-Cocaine, Tobacco, Hydro-Marijuana, Hashish, Heroin, Angel Dust, Morphine, Amphetamine, Magic Mushroom, use in our bed, unless: [War-Time-Study-Permitted]: I was asking woman to grow with me in love, because we have to. More than that because

I wanted her to. Learning to love. I heard she died of complications to the human body, the tailbone, the skin, the head, the right breast, the right eardrum, the exorcism and the flush, because of a love for pain, and a patience for illness. I just wanted you to know that I was thinking of you, and that I love you never.

A year ago, I wrote a short diary writing about me and my ambitions, my ideas, my travels to The United States and Italy. It ended within a hundred pages. "Diary in Debt!", it was called. I lived in prophecy for a year before writing. It ended in Los Angeles, California. Shortly after the Malibu fire. I was in Venice Beach, after spending a week in Redondo Beach, when the truth showed me time that had already happened and killed people, because of what I was studying. People are presently failing in acts of love and humanity. Some argue I was possessed by scriptures. A failure of happiness because of my own faults in which I deserved to suffer. I like to think I was exposed to the truth of a young child's body being destroyed in violation, for more money, guiltless power, a way to teach me that what I care for will suffer. To remind me of how I will listen, and do what I am told. To obey. Then, to obey what, besides sickness. Eccentric, mature, authoritative, control to show intelligence. They want humility, and for you to have the will to accept that they will always be more powerful than you. Parenting and challenging a mind convinced, that it was blessed to torment my children with pain and death so that they understand rules.

When I returned to Toronto, I practiced and arranged music for the record. When it started, the prophecy, I was on my way to the library when I was introduced to a child, and other children dying in violation and trying to survive on their own time, without a sacrifice. They wished my company as their dad. I started a record with them, at that time it was called "United States at War". We started as a family, working on my book, and the record, to earn money to be together, I was going to be their Dad, and they accepted.

One afternoon in Santa Monica, I was tanning, lying on the beach, taking my time, a young Man with a good chance in starting a family, a relationship with a Woman, continued working on the record that preoccupied me from being broke on the street, a war of more than ten years of living outside homeless, single, unemployed, uncomfortable rooming houses, and uncompleted high school education. I used to be so ambitious and fairly disciplined with music. Writing, always writing, working on prophecies to be published. That day in Santa Monica, I had the power to witness financial success in music, so I started to produce "Chord of a United States Pin!". Played with it for a year, produced to a lock, equipped for a world tour. Added an EP, "Vabe Singer!". Became "*Varadero Beach: - Live off the Floor at Airport Runway!". I started writing to earn money to begin my career as a musician for a band called Cuba changed to Italia. Changed to Tropical Alien. I submitted that diary and was responded to within a few days, with a handwritten return mail from the publishing house. Their answer was 'not interested'. I started laughing and said to myself, "They made a bad mistake listening to women."

I was advised to work with an agent. Within days, response from agent, 'not interested'. I mailed to two other publishers since then. No response yet. It's been a year, and close to a decade since the reinvention of psychology, witnessing my life as a prophecy. Mazares, destiny strong enough for prophecies to write about. Well, here I live then, with more than faith to keep praying all day as I did when I was a young and ambitious teenage boy. With responsibilities and work to be done, what exactly is it to pray all day. I like to talk with the power of life, the Sun, the Moon, and the Earth. About justice, protection, rules, love, corrupt intercourse, parenting, pleasure, business, money, healing, and drugs. Convinced that I have become a professional pharmaceutical drug user. Believing that in my time praying, it is wise to be *Selective with Drugs*.

Judgment of wealth is so vicious in my life, for I have barely nothing but a power in prayer, and an immortal family, with four wives and children, protected. I should be careful with how I spell nothing, my energy was treated, and my life was worked to the power of growth. In this case, there was a time in prayer sacrifice, that I noticed money to earn. Also, there was the absence of being a dad, a husband, a friend, a relative. An educated heart for drugs, alcohol, and food. The way you agree to separate from people because you admit that there's a difference that has to be given time to or there will be a judgment of wrath from the heavens to annihilate everyone.

Acknowledge the permission you allow to thinking that the human race is unified as one, under the influence of legal drugs. I thought I was smart when choosing to use pharmaceutical drugs that are guiltless. I swore to never study illegal Cocaine casually again, until further mandatory notice. The night I did, while my diary was in the mail, on the way to New York City, Mazares, the much-anticipated prophet, who traveled from reincarnation United States of America, to work this life for money with show business, politics, sports, seeds, resources, heartbeat food, construction, family, and natural causes.

Ready to begin a return to music, with a new power since last leaving to mature as an adult conducting stage business. It's not funny how I was stubbornly convinced that prophecies I studied about me were exorcism violations rather than me misbehaving to see and hear warnings. Possessively, continuing bad habits that violate in the body would be the suicidal way. Without breaking the law out loud, I want to talk about how there was a previous misery in private during an exorcism studying illegal activity with crack-cocaine, and lsd-acid. Tired of all the excuses, not to see the truth in death with illegal drug use. MagicMushrooms are becoming legal.

Years ago, when I was younger, before acknowledging guilt, yet afraid to die without love for someone, a woman. Being denied entrance into heaven terrified me. I felt obligated to do something for people who like to see and hear of proof that there is love after life, during life, responsible for life. Inspiration to ignore choices that would have made life more difficult to live. When you're young and ambitious, developing your own style, it's good to forget all the *False-Warnings: Ignore the Betrayal* with all and lovers to a left sided man *A White Man stranger who offers gifts, fortune, and fame. Defeating Saturn. After they sell themselves to pleasure with tax protected life, (*Stage business, music, films, publishing, sports,*) sex, impregnating women, children, and family. I just wanted you to know that I was thinking of you, and that I love you always.

When a living human being can be responsible for tempting you for years by agreeing to, and *sharing with the idea of you failing* in test to righteousness, tries to show you wisdom, providing love and truth, strength and human decency, through friendship. Money is precious again, the way it was when giving time to other people, who at that time were to a left-sided Woman.

I like admitting that I need the Sun, Moon, and Earth's energy. Along with being a Man, every day. Besides myself. Women will always be my love in bonding. And in corrupt, explicit intercourse. Men who are not gay, who need Men is where I have been ever since I left a basement in Greece, and a wooden band I was in with four other Men in 13,784,262. Making music history. Quit the band, because after four years rehearsing seven days a week, five or more hours every night, I smoked tobacco instead of drinking tea and cough syrup. My voice wasn't improving fast enough. I was a DJ in the making, before stardom, for how convinced I was that there was something behind my weak voice and lame stage presence. In case you looked to see, there were extensive hours of me and my mind alone with the Sun, Moon, and Earth, concerned as to exactly what it was that interested destiny in having me passionate for fine arts, voice and vocal. Without enough skill. As I was there mistakenly rehearsing with tobacco instead of tea, alive, existing. Is there something in this life that you expected from me, as labor that involved anything other than being in prayer for myself and other people while composing? Luckily, I was convinced that there was prophetic power that I had, that would be used by someone other than myself, millions of people. That I also knew.

One night, I was stubborn about being remembered for resisting temptation, for fearing the fire of all heaven's wrath, not because it will hurt, but because it's not normal to be in love with failing in temptation. I was in a bar, ordered a glass of red wine, and began writing a letter to a friend, telling of my premonition of death, so that when they received the mail, I would have prophesied my death because of my blessings with heaven. And to remember all my stubbornness with objecting to wickedness. I mailed it, and walked home on the highway, it was nighttime.

When I arrived home alive, I believed that I had dealt to myself a life that was willing to be an example, if necessary, to other people about energy existing, and the wrath upon it if it fails to rules abiding peace with other people. Death sentences, I have no sympathy for, or argument for if they were deserved. Humans killing humans in war. I have agreed to what the dead and dying in guilt, deserve.

What is it that has a young man more interested in convincing you of explicit sex energy with more than one woman and selection with drugs? At 19, I knew that spirits did reincarnate as other people, with different names. I saw the option to consult thousand-year-old temples guiding energies since the beginning of time. When your defensive strategy has obligations to do with violated immaturity and mutilation. Authority and more authority.

What is it then about aliens that have a traveling U.F.O. said to be true, not true. I produced a record with circle lettuce and tax protection wrath one night, next day 44 houses missing. This being my debut in stage business, as a

DJ. Ambition that deserves money for the work it did for the earth and people.

Sun, Moon, and Earth. I need the strength to plow ten acres of cornfield with my bare hands, thank you Mazares, for allowing me to be heard.

Energetic people understand me when it was either Figuras, sex, or myself in prayer. I did pray for a relationship with love to keep me company as a heterosexual Man praying to understand life with providing natural causes. Responsible to provide a healing power for people interested teaches me something about energies among me while I was young, a small boy with nothing but wisdom to play. With respect to parenting, where deserved, is it not worth it to think that there is work on this planet, fortune in providing love and healing. Importantly, raising with assistance to judge the wicked and good.

For instance, in the court of law, you're not allowed to be guilty, or you'll be punished. Study and remind yourself, how you choose to have no guilt with your own actions. Rio De Janeiro, my destination with money to complete an arrangement of dance electronica music. Before I was born there was disco. I listened to it when I was younger. I listened to it now a lot more than I ever did, especially over the last year.

Studied all morning until afternoon. Walked into the city, to make money, [War-Time]: on the sidewalk, to buy a ticket to a Major League Baseball game home opener. Made the money, walked to the stadium to buy a ticket, sold out. Bought a bottle of red wine, visited a friend, and watched the baseball game on projection television. Made a promise to listen to baseball games on radio this season.

Add work to my progress recording and production with music if I listen to baseball games on radio. Televised baseball and recorded footage of previous World Series games on my black and white television also worked. More powerful than regular season games, leading to championship. Black and White baseball is a production secret that I use when making records. Walked to buy a bottle of red wine. "Babies with a Handgun!", new album title.

Prayed for power to bring peace to the human child, using music and stage. First time I arranged to write for publishing, it was worked over from morning to early night. I finished it within a week. A more casual approach this time, considering the production work on the records during the day and night. I like to take my walk into the heart of the city to make money for my red wine. Not interested in tying myself to my room to finish without drugs and alcohol. Tonight, I have time to think and type.

Yesterday, I thought of being involved in a concert as a music performance. That's where I always wanted to be; on stage, in concert, in prayer, for myself, and for people who like to pray for a blessed life, forgiveness, healing, investigative prayer is good too. I like to see and hear confessions in the energy while praying, the answer solves all confusion. I must have prayed for my life suspecting death without failure, at least a number of times a day, when I was young. I still do; not as worried about dying on the way out of the bar by a band of bullets and knives unless I'm guilty. Try another bar if it's destined for a terrorist attack.

Understanding the work of prophecy as exorcism makes life easier to prevent death that would have happened. My strongest prayer with other people has to be during concerts, as a Sun, Moon, and Earth worshiper with a landed U.F.O. in New York City, New York, United States Of America.

Today, I wanted to perform a song at a concert and record it. It's funny how most of the work produced is done by praying while working. It really is a position to be credited as much as corrupt sex with other lovers. It becomes a heterosexual perfection. Providing a clean guiltless prayer, is just as important as powerful corrupt heterosexual sex in the ass. I prefer to think of it that way, or else it becomes personal and intimidating, thinking that other people fail to leave their jobs, families and sex life to build a prayer in the desert.

Psychic power, when I play with time. Made money for a bottle of red wine, made more for a meal. Trouble with energy today.

I was answered in prayer earlier this morning, and was told to work the powers that compensate the human being for being violated aggressively by other energies. Either left uncared for, to be troubled by people who struggle with peace, as an inclusion to punishment or forgiven and told to add protection in prayer due to an energy failure.

On Saturday, there is violence with energy. You're allowed to pray for other people if you want. As long as you're not being taken by a power of temptation to heal the undeserving wicked. They need their rehabilitation time, time to repent for themselves, to prevent themselves from being hurt. By life, they eventually have to find the power to work along with other people.

The relationship between a human being and infinite power does involve the disciplinary truth, who has responsibility for your life. Two people, childbirth, powering another human being, responsible for that child or left bludgeoned in a violent accident. Other than your own will to provide work in life, someone else is responsible for you. Then, politics for me becomes tax protected, committed to responsibility, for children as well as adults.

Living in North America, without a job, a girlfriend, money, friends, living in hostels, different rooming houses, and outside. People are judging everyday whether you did nothing good for yourself or other people yesterday. Ten years of this life in public, broke, without sex, adds to ideas that think to kill or at least beat. I lived this way, while praying all day. Knowing that I was not one who was hostile to women, families, husbands, and the employed. I had to find faith in believing what I was thinking, without guilt.

I decided to concentrate on prayer for good reasons, education and employment ignored, so that I could power a prayer instead of anything else. Eventually, with instinct earned, you begin to convince yourself that corruption is trying to control your life to spend money on illegal drug deals.

When I started noticing that life was economically trained so that I would spend no money on certain businesses and people. I knew that I was being gambled into a blessed way of life. By the prophetic nature of The White Man in London, New York City, Philadelphia, Wall Street, Chicago, San Francisco, Pittsburgh, Santa Fe, Reno, and Las Vegas, literally.

It is true; the probability of me spending money that my responsible life, impregnating me into earth, disagreed with, forced a working against me. I remember wasting money when I was younger.

I immediately flew to English-Rome when I suspected controlling English-Rome was in my destiny. Power followed me during the weekend in Milan, when I was there. Just adding to my young suspicions of being born with ancient Roman-Pompeii powers. Another prayer was answered for me this morning, to help the way I use my defensive and condemning United-Kingdom skills. It was a good answer too. Useful. So useful, I can concentrate on being closer to perfect, without contemplating and hesitating while taking the life of a human being who deserved it.

Walked downtown to buy a bottle of red wine to have with ice. Walked downtown again to work for [War-Timed] money to buy a bottle of red wine. I work outside because I read all day, at night I write. I collect social assistance. X-rays showed violations, being punctured and mutilated. Provincial financial security. My rent is paid, I'll have $568.00 dollars a month for myself. I drank all the grape juice wine that I fermented. When I need wine, I work. Consider it cash for energy work. I knew when I was making money on the power of the sidewalk, that I was learning how to control the power to pray, plus other energies, like reading, writing, and music. No suicide. To tip the Zyden of White Man Land, for a taste of his power has its rewards. You're allowed to provide in the power of a team. A tax protection team power. A tax protection prayer. Depending on prayer allows you to be forgiven, blessed and allowed to live, resisting temptation, then here I work as a businessman, selling my power of prayer to you. The listeners of music can pray too, if they like, especially about the voice and vocal cord. It's always a good idea to pray about forgiveness. Psychologically, it's good to know that you spent your time productively, working the energy into heaven, with other people, or by yourself. I heard a young child once pray to me, asking me if I wanted to be their dad.

"We'll look for a mom," they said, so that we could be in a family. I promised that I would personally do something about it. When I noticed the people trying to kill them before they were with me, their dad, I invested all my faith in prayer, and control of destiny, to keep them alive until we were together with each other. Eventually, the trickery with using voices of children that never existed ended.

I was trying to stay close to heaven. There were other children there; happy children. They said I could be their dad if I still wanted to. I did. They're with me now every day. I want them to know that I'm thinking of them, and that I love them always. I love their Mom too. It's prophecy that I have to be with them this way. Single parenting. There's no other choice. I want to be honest with you and tell you that I believe, those children that I made my own, were there to give me what I wanted in a family while I was praying, during the day, at night, on foot, on vacation. The world was busy at work. And I was praying. Considering my destiny as a writer, a DJ-sequence programmer, it should be good. A potential published writer with the ambition to record music with money to buy his children a towel to soak their violated blood, and mutilated guts, next time I see a Zombie earning a living next to my child's left arm, head, and heart. I saved money and bought something I'd like to kill you with. Believe, this is a *WARNING*.

Stayed in and made myself learn how to be strict with prayer, controlling my own life. Before the end of the night, I wanted to write.

Studied assassinations on DVD today. Started watching it yesterday. Truly, with where I am now in this book, writing, I've mentioned it before, the confusion of penalty vs prophecy. In case, it ever was to be the penalty of death for reasons. Count work and blessings. Prophecies, reason for the living to live good, for acceptance in heaven. Entering heaven at the time of bleeding to death has a lot to do with wanting to feel it. You want to suffer as I kill you with the Sun, Moon, and Earth. The power to walk out of the body, then into heaven, without pain, before being killed for no reason, I disagree with it. Let it be known that I want to challenge the idea of using the body as an investigation to be killed, gambling that you walk out of the body before the pain of being killed. Possessed bravery, instigated by the news of entering heaven at the time of death without natural causes.

It's a good idea to be selective with voices, to assume that listening to telepathic voices is not the best idea for everybody, regardless of the success and reputation, would be the best idea. A blessing happened with time, reward, and money.

Bought a bottle of red wine. As much as I may have been convinced in the past that there was special power in my prayer, I sure was awakened by how special it was, and how it had to stay that way. I was hit badly by The

[EXORCISM LEAK TELEPATHY GANG] Zombie, with an abusive, life-threatening, blood drawn experience that made me undoubtedly believe that I was more important than I thought, and needed to live life more seriously, as if other people were aware of my powers. No longer, just ideas and obedient worship to survive. You can't live like this with other people bothering you with cocaine, tobacco, marijuana, hashish, hydroponics, crack-cocaine, angel dust, acid, morphine, amphetamine, whiskey, tomato sauce, heroin, turkey, peaches, and horse meat. I was excited about cashing the money for the book I was writing when I studied the coming of Mazares at the library. That was ten years ago. My ambition to imagine a party paid by myself after being published, influenced by arresting. Seconds later, a steel toe boot kicked my mouth and lips in a holding cell. I knew that choosing to stop guilty illegal drug use and dealing started my enemies gambling that I would be sacrificed by rabbis, priests, and imam's without heaven's permission. Who are they talking to? Planning to kill without permission. The Mongoloid, The Woman, The Man, The Negroid, The Australoid and The Caucasian. Phone me at 583 351 9340. I'm willing to talk to you about it.

Yesterday, I was praying while listening to music on my portable cd player. While praying, I thought of asking if there was anything that invited the power of life into the Planet Earth for solutions to my problem. The prayer answered "Giving you; your room!"

Believe that arrested by the law is up to the discretion of the Police department. If you're homeless and they think it's time to rest in a government institution where they have powers circulating, like proper sorcery and witchcraft, casting good spells and healing you while in jail. I was arrested due to exhaustion living on the street, after a year homeless in Little Italy.

When I was acquitted and released, I was lucky to find a room in Little Italy as an English-Rome, where I could rest in a bed, with a bathtub and shower, and electricity to use if necessary. I was in jail waiting for my trial during The World Cup when Italy won.

I was awakening from rest, when a vision of Alexander Hamilton, The Sun, The Moon, and The Earth appeared in my room like a giant big screen television broadcasting him from The Oval Office, ready to give a speech. His voice started to sound like it does through a speaker. The speech, specifically for me, "Mazares, you have to believe what I'm going to tell you, without thinking that it's a distraction to prevent you from being powerful without guilt. This isn't an illusion trying to make you sick of Alexander Ham[BURGER]ilton, I'm really trying to help you. The garage where you sometimes go to barbecue. At the back of the house in the laneway. While you're in the garage, leaning against the car, slightly to the side of the passenger window near the wheel well. A Zombie is planning on breaking through the windshield with someone hiding in the car. The people on the outside of the car will feed you to the person in the front seat. You get pulled into the car with your torso on the hood. They unzip your pants, pull them down to your knees, then they start cutting your scrotum, to pull out the testicles by hand and shove them down your throat while the other cuts through your eyeballs. Then, a cut from the middle of your neck down to the belly button, digging your anatomy out with a knife. If you don't go, it won't happen."

I went somewhere else to barbecue. I was on the patio, on the second floor near my room, in the back of the house, facing the laneway. Not a move without psychic fortune-telling, palm-reading, intelligence using cacti. I prepared a charcoal bed, pitched a light, and started placing the cow and chicken on the barbecue grill. While waving the hot charcoal, I felt my bones, muscles, nerves, veins, and skin, dying the way they would have if I went to the garage. I stopped all cigarette smoking after that. Started going to the library. Was introduced to the future of having children. Eventually ended up in California, decided to go back to show business 24 hours a day, and finish the book I wanted to write.

In this room, the room I'm in now, the good choice is, I haven't done anything wrong since I've been here. When I thought about the room after the trial with cigarettes that Novera Novo prefers not to smoke unless Creator makes him, it was a test and surely a last chance for me to be more selective with habits, before being terribly hurt by someone. Good that I believed that permission to be selective has more power with respect amongst Earth's Nature rather than worry about being a sudden protest to Creation. Protest against Infinity has to be destined for a burial.

Next, after touring "Radia Olaview!" when it's finished recording and arranging, there's an idea. It's called "Ozera, you have to control your own love!" A sentence that works through both part I and part II of an ap. Radia Olaview has to be understood as the recording that allowed me to confront my relationship with whom I pray to, intentions to invent the human Caucasian male's existence without inviting wickedness into the life or room where he rests and has explicit bed sex. It doesn't feel like there's that much love there anymore. I'd like to ask for more than forgiveness. A chance to be respected as I used to be, because of habits that convince me have to stop. In relation to punishment and prophecy, I was told in prayer yesterday, that my fortune to continue living and growing, rather than being killed, was a blessing of favoritism. Based on that conversation in prayer, expect this recording project to strengthen my energies with responsibility, punishment, exorcism, unclog, drain, filter and flush. It already has, hours later, destined me for the Rocky Mountains, Colorado, U.S.A.; Added to Kentucky Mountains, so did the title, from "You will climb Rocky Mountains!" to "Control your own love!". Told to be the controversial project of my career. Better to take care of it now, then to struggle at the release date and tour after.

Based on events, possible bodily harm, assault, accidental misfortune, the study of punishment and 1-studying, is the answer in: "Ozera, you have to control your own love". I'm convinced that stopping expensive unproductive habits like smoking tobacco cigarettes, and hydroponic marijuana, started an interest in living properly.

To indulge in pleasure. A handgun, I was told to buy and use even if I pray and believe in energy punishment. Witnessing a fulfillment of prophecies, involving weapons and missiles, and lots of people dying by the thousands as I was in prayer about life, and life not deserved. Prayed all day, spent time with four different Figuras for four hours.

Radia Olaview sails to Australia with money earned from 'Defending Alive: Coming of Mazares Dead!'

Bought red grape juice to ferment in my room. Obeying the strongest order in prayer I ever heard. Last chance to be forgiven with what I did to the inside of my body. To the nightclub to disco with whiskey or legal mushrooms..

Worked on my book called "Dreaming with Camera Paparazzi!" This book's ambition is to travel in a time machine and kill the guilty with the power side of George Washington.

If you believe in improper sorcery and witchcraft, I had my fair share of it, against my will to sing and simply didn't deserve a recording contract. After six years with slow improvement, I figured I would keep praying considering the private happenings. I'll keep listening to music though, and I did. Every day with headphones, when I moved out of the house, into the hostels and the sidewalk for 15 years.

Love to be paid for writing. Money is a quick example of reward for doing good in life, because I don't have a lot, and never really did for the longest time. Money in the arts, at the beginning, $ N.O.T $ pay every week right away. It can be dangerous if your lifestyle's being judged, single, not working, and continuing in the same schedule for years; more than ten. People spy, people notice. No strong relationships with anyone but the Sun, Moon, and Earth. Habits that did nothing but slow me down, was a bad idea. It still feels like I lost my respect coming from power. People play with me from time to time, reminding me of what it could be like to be appreciated by The Nature Of The Round World, rather than neglected by [EXORCISM LEAK TELEPATHY GANGS]. Then they leave. Leaving troubled energy, to remind me of the burial process of the mind being attacked, trying and failing terribly to condemn right away using defensive powers. Energy failing with weakness, temptation is surrendering to everything, every opportunity to have you bleed to death, agreeing to it, without any will to survive at all. Then there's enough heart in you to remember you were once favored, in prayer for life, with happenings, and love, and it could end because you had to get involved with a prophecy that you were warned about. Thinking the love you knew existed would be strong enough to save you and it isn't. Living outside, no money left, prayers are sounding filthy from wicked thoughts in the wind violating, trying to disguise and hide. You knew they did, contemplating death, suspected warning, but they did it anyway. People are spying to kill, the sidewalk's cracked cement is stained dirty. Your pockets are empty, with a growing instinct about people violating. Maybe they'll live, maybe they won't, feeling the Moon's disapproval with ignorance to warning. Keeping to yourself while using legal drugs becomes trivial as to what I did in life to deserve a doubt with survival. {Because this is a book and not a test, and memory is critical. Broken Defense = Contemplation with survival. Reason for broken defense = Telepathic trafficking and possession and failure to flush an exorcism.}

Until tomorrow, to do it again. Another five to six years of this, losing blood from hits on the street. Knowing that the highest hands in heavens had to be called for bleeding. Possibly then that the money was not permitted because of the habits with legal drugs. Not intending to make the same mistake again. Lucky my honesty with intentions to be in prayer under the influence of legal drugs was more powerful and sincere than an addiction to using legal drugs. Foolish now, when you think of it, assuming normality in authority and mutilation when using legal drugs to heal, pray, and meditate. Praying under the influence of legal drugs with peaceful intentions. Ignoring safety can still get you killed. More than convinced that all this knowledge and relationship with power that I have, will eventually be gifted and granted wealth to pursue something more than ideas. To be in prayer is also inspiration from the highest power in life. To make powerful music without losing interest in political science or economics. The mind, studied enough to control a nation, used to arrange seven notes, guarantees an award someday. Plus, I add power of prayer to the arrangement and recording, the way they did to the Synagogue, Vatican, and Mecca. Politics then is a campaign with interests to pray in [THE PYRAMIDS AND THE SPHINX] different places. The qualified are powerful enough to appeal to all people while religious to their preferences. A sporting event ends that way. Was good for all, better for some people, making more money for some people, while others made less. With this power that I've invited for myself to live comfortably with judgment that kills people guilty, will in fact be a threat to some people even if it's peaceful and in love with prayer. Good thing is, I'll always be interested in being accepted into heaven to live immortally. Walking off the field without the cup, every time, has its trouble with me as well. When it's available to be won, I would rather win it, then settle for life in heaven as an immortal. An energy sore, a weak loser, I don't have these troubles. The night I held my blood from drowning me on the sidewalk for asking for drugs to smoke convinces me that I did more than win that night, with above average good choices. By the fifth incident drawing blood and the prophecies of bloody accidents I understood an answered prayer means to resist and be (selective) with drugs, music, film, publication, sports, politics, economics, women, food, and clothing.

I started to write this to be paid for what it was that I thought I had done for myself and other people since the day I was born. Faithful to the lesson about luck with money my whole life, teaching me to spend wisely when choosing to medicate the inside of my body. To believe that a power in your life, lifeline, prayed for permission to torment and abuse the psychology of itself as another human being about health. To prevent a prophecy of wasting a life spent using illegal cocaine and other illegal drugs preferred not to use.

At, 08:37:00 a.m. in the morning on Thursday, May, 06, 13,784,276. I vow to never use the drugs that I was told not to use while instinctively choosing to pray as my ambition in life. Solving an uncomfortable judgment of death in my life that I left when I was younger. Ambition as a recording artist.

Never seemed to find a general happiness with what I was doing, until I retreated back to thinking about the Sun, Moon, and the Earth. I now know the difference between prophecy and condemnation. Prayed for the strength to build a private school, if I was to ever be published and recorded. Studied prayer. At night, I had a good conversation in prayer. I was told I would never be killed unless I ignored a warning about being guilty.

'Ozera, you have to control your own love'. DJ Novera, new album title. The wisdom of my life has grown from basic knowledge of energy, to witnessing and hearing the future of the dead in war, or natural causes. Human beings, responsible for nothing but temptation. If necessary, I could strike a nation from the sky to have them destroyed without assistance from anyone but myself.

This life has intentions to destroy human life which failed to live by expectations. Studied, blessed, and worked for Military Intelligence, to secure my life, and other people's.

Studied prayer. Prayed for my life on a few occasions, worried that it would be taken without heaven's blessings. I prayed for forgiveness because it didn't feel like I was going to be forgiven. Thinking back to that night, when I was a victim of choices, intending to kill, I was smoking tobacco cigarettes and hydro-marijuana. Since then, I've stopped. It doesn't happen to me the same way anymore.

I laugh now, merry with my drink and sane with my drugs. Too bad I thought it was crimes of humanity, when it was nothing more than me being an idiot to life and what it has to offer to someone who knows that drink and drug will serve you well, and good to better, if done properly. I like the luck praying while I'm drinking beer with ice. It's like I knew there was a heart in heaven who believed it the way I do. Lots of drink, lots of drugs, lots of explicit sex, lots of food, technology, and here we have a place called Paradise On Earth.

I thought about you dying of natural causes most of the time, stranger or good friend. I just wanted you to know that I was thinking of you, and that I love you always. The wicked, they'll be taken care of righteously, by the order of Heaven. Studied control of prayer. A handshake on the street. A handshake on the street to symbolize a commitment to singing, last week, a handshake to symbolize a commitment to DJ in a merchant's place.

I was given my children back, after losing them the night I chose a cup of choices, to be under the influence and using a drug that I was told, and knew, was a ruling against and not an illusion or betrayal.

Tanned in the sun while reading. Started a red wine business. Was answered in a prayer for power to ferment grape juice into wine. Red wine. To working. A long time since I worked with ideas that produce a sound recording art.

If it were important for me to be there, a signed recording artist, I would have been before, when I was younger, and fairly disciplined with rehearsing and ambition. The skill could have been perfected. Starting with a sacrifice of drinking tea. smoking grass and pot, Gum weed. Success is using gum weed. Stubborn to see tobacco as medicine, I failed in resisting for what the tobacco cigarette had against me, specifically, same with the adding of fire through the mouth, working down the throat, to the voice. A waste of time, to answer prayers that are destroyed by habits. Considering my decisions to try DJ'ing, I haven't smoked tobacco for over a year now and choose to never do so again, until further mandatory notice. What I did do this past weekend is experience a life of strength, using drugs. This, I have been comfortable with, since the start of a new year.

Intravenously, using legal drugs that work well with me is the best time I've ever had in life. If you're comfortable using drugs, and never tried injecting, into a vein with more work, you're missing masculine supremacy, with sincerely, enough power to completely drown out all the wickedness that tempts and haunts you. I'm willing to take full responsibility for recommending the idea. Show business is a little funny to me, the way they overdose everything that ever went anywhere near it. I prefer life with intravenous drugs. In my prayers, I add the power to be published so that I could have money to do more than I do now. To invest in a music project, then to tour. It's an old prayer that I've had, to be paid as a writer and a musician.

Yesterday, I bought a pail of red grape juice to ferment in my room. My promise and agreement with the highest hand in nature, with red wine, is to be the beginning of forgiveness, and the start of a life with wealth, pursuing ambitions in the arts.

What is it exactly that tempts a Man, or a Woman to aggravate a power with whom you know from scriptures and prayer as a power that will destroy, kill, torture, and torment in psychological abuse and fear. My answer was misunderstanding exorcism from prophecy. Sincerity and truth in the mind has opportunity to lie. I was failing to differentiate prophecy from troubled exorcism, and was neglected the money and power I needed to pursue any ambitions that I had, previous to reincarnating. Corruption with healing can be slightly uncomfortable. Insight and instinct, or corruption in healing. A good way to look at it is, a corrupt exorcism is a prophecy about renting a room in Colorado and spending the money.

38

Remember, my life was prophesied by Nostradamus, a psychic fortune teller. To see me alive, in power with genius; an audience was there. This means that work in the heavens has already adjusted destiny in my favor, with skill and permission to earn money as an artist musician. It's been 35 years of worshiping sounds and music, arranging notes and lyrics. Listening, working, creating, and designing albums that heal intellects and provide power of prophecy. I was prescribed to a hospital bed with an overnight stay that lasted a month. Recommended mental disability. To be hired as a mental disability compared to other applicants. What is it then, this life with medical history? Illness in the mind, living in hostels; homeless, broke, unemployed, and shifting from rooming house to rooming house.

What it is then that the heavens have decided to do, besides, torture in a Roswell Cage. Humiliating, insulting, playing with my acknowledgement of power that I see, happenings I experience, prophecies of my work in music, with a public that does nothing but assume that I am worth a room to test with basic shelter and wealth. Surviving in consequence to trouble, responsible for 35 years of age. The last 15, without association with family or friends that I used to have.

When I was young, my temptation with wickedness made me feel like I was tested and winning. The life like this now, is improving with choices, drugs, food, alcohol, fabric, and women, like no other human being would ever believe. It truly is. If I'm published with this new version, after being denied with what I wrote last year, it would then be genius to an idea that was meant to heal the world.

Worked on wine business, recording music, and producer business. Paid for business cards. Opened a business phone line. Made number and business available to the public by visiting in person, and using advertisement boards in music instrument shops. Mazares is praying for a show of money, with either red wine, writing, or the producing. To make matters more sensible for success, I have a phone number activated for business with promotion, advertising, and marketing plans.

To start Radia Olaview, (DJ Novera's bedroom) part I and II. If there's a heart that serves justice to what's deserved without unfair play, then I should be phoned at 538 351 9340, any day now. If not, then there was work to do the way life is, broke with a prayer, and an obligation to provide natural causes. A bed, room, with $100.00 a week. Surrendered to prayer. For strength in witnessing people killed in war. Surrendered to prayer, for power to convince women that Chicago, (Go Blackhawks!), my guitars, and my turntables work with trains to enforce heterosexual love. Began working on song ideas with my voice, intending to be accompanied by music arranged by computer software. Followed the same choices as Thursday; praying for forgiveness with condemned money a few feet away. Not close enough to be poor, so working without it. Vocal training using headphones and previously recorded material.

During the night, I had a break from singing. Reached into the bar in my room, to open another bottle of red wine, with headphones off and music paused. I heard an energy playback of the song, I was working on, from the start to finish. At the next drink of red wine, I drank in celebration of being a recording artist, agreed to by the energies. For I just listened to a version of myself singing a song that was not recorded with technology, just rehearsed out loud. I was granted power to have my music recorded on tape with energy, this means then that money will be granted, made from cotton, to finish a copy for the flesh.

A blessing of money happened to me. It included other people who were there with me, listening. It was an increase from 100 to 100,000 people. My ambition was blessed by the heavens and all that has powered life for the work that I had done with my power from prayer good. The people were happy, and we were told of the persecution that is to come to those who failed us, with greed for money.

Proposed an opportunity to energetic people. To invest in The Florida Islands tape; a relationship power tape. A Woman for Man tape.

Last night before rehearsal, I was challenged by some strange energies to do something other than work. I turned to the existing people outside of planet Earth and offered them a chance to reincarnate on planet earth. Advertising the human life. Strategy of WW3 victory, understanding trains, subways, buses, streetcars, and children that have been bruised for too long.

Allowed to spend seven months working on debut, ambition recording, and a good witness was time, to what I was doing while single and broke, powerful enough to read energies into a ditch at any given time of the day, especially for suicide after a warning, strengthening family, providing natural causes, internet, and the left rib. Love!

Never intended to have any guilt to hear of death including those who deserved it either. Considering my witness to temptation, I preferred to be in prayer where it was safe, without any reason to ever leave. Sub-zero weather in the winter, walking miles to dinner at night, starting from early in the morning for breakfast, I was closer to war with nature's enemies then I ever was.

I smartened near the end of my punishment, stopped assuming that drugs and alcohol were meant to be used by everyone.

I used places like the library and developed a schedule to self-educate, considering the schooling wasn't important enough to pay close attention to; never strong enough to pass into a secure job. As life develops, the future may argue that time educated me under the influence of headphones in class. I was always too preoccupied with show business, or too interested in being somewhere else, like Hollywood, California.

Then, I think of how many times an individual has a physical confrontation with a stranger. That's not a boxing ring. That's a sidewalk. The relationship in prayer turned on me and made me bleed, more than once. Psychologically, Heaven. Love. Judging my peacefulness with sincerity. There's no way I'm condemned for the likes of other people. I was a victim of irresponsibility. The Sun, Moon, and Earth are going to beat me as a plan to teach drug use and controlling an exorcism to the future watching is what I thought.

Thousands of people killed in an act of wrath; watching the news briefing at breakfast, the next morning. I heard the news as a blanket to my own psychology, threatened on the street. I was sure to add my love in prayer again with smoke, fire, and drugs.

At 21, I was of equal power to the most powerful Caesar's of Rome. I knew, because I was blessed to understand that I was. Heaven and weapon, with what they do to people in private who later become known for having power, is that they're to be known as powerful. I was uncomfortable leaving prayer. So I walked. Stayed out of trouble, thought about dying of natural causes with the rest of the living world who deserved to do the same. From 21 to mid-34, I was left without the wealth of a Ceasar, because of negotiable allergies with wine, marijuana, tobacco cigarettes, ginger-ale, tomato sauce, wheat and pork,

Once my left calf was up for breakfast, as long as there was a sidewalk long enough to stay awake with me, I would walk it. Planning writing to be published. A book about a Man who prayed for publishing money while writing and providing natural causes, to then record music, once paid. I can hear my family with children blessed by the power responsible for life. I lived my life, from this day on, knowing that The Florida Islands would be the answer to every Man's life who hears, use the true existence of aliens, and selected drug use.

Better to work and be with my family. In the last year and a half, there's been written witness to there being nothing less than a thousand dollars a month. Not a fair pay for a published writer. As soon as I decided to write a book for money a few years ago, after spying homeless in the late spring, summer, and early fall. On my way to the library, I was blessed with a parenting relationship. My children were introduced to me. Blessed as a dad, blessed as a family, and blessed with prophecy to what was intending to end our lives. Not too much money, yet I do like to admit without guilt that my children were introduced to me, blessed as a dad, blessed as a family, blessed with prophecy for what was ending our lives. Not too much money, yet I do like to admit without guilt that my relationship with my children brought the most peaceful life I've ever experienced and will continue to be. Understood that heaven and 'Gaul's Law' has changed to a sex law that will inherit the planets. I started today, yesterday, days ago. I passed the last of my tests, agreeing to multiple heterosexual bonded partners for sex. Without failing in temptation to be sexual without child birth. I love my children, my bondage, and my wives. I'm thinking about them, and I love them, always. Like anyone else, it's in my best interest to love the idea of being a romantic and being alive, since I was answered in prayer about who and where to pray to on Sunday. I noticed millions of other people, thinking that their lives were intended to be Catholic. I study my religion using music, in the powers of the Sun, Moon, and Earth.

Last night, I was working for money to replace a DVD player to watch movies that got destroyed last month while I was watching something. Before closing, I walked to an electronic shop to buy a new one. I did this with paying for the other half, with the money I saved from being paid monthly by the government. It's already saved to be spent tonight at the nightclub. As I was choosing a product, from the outside on the sidewalk, looking through the window, I walked in to buy it. Walked to the window display, picked one, handed it to a sales representative, and demonstrated the power of mechanics on a television for sale, showing cable. I agreed to pay watching, as it was working with DVD inserted and playing to show. I paid for it and left with a new DVD player. I talked with my children about the sale, shortly after I was in control of Filmmaking Technology intelligence. A technological happening.

Making [DJ *Novera] Novo*, both of The Florida Islands, recording artist. DJ-sequence programmer and wooden wind band singer. Technologically educated with JVC, by Alien lives on older planets. Prayed to be trusted with never using again what was told not to use. Prayed for forgiveness, for punishment to end. Writing now at 07:30:00 a.m. in the morning for the first time since Thursday afternoon. I will have to go back and write for the days of Friday to Sunday. On Wednesday afternoon, I played guitar in a music shop intending to buy an amplifier so that I could rehearse and arrange music while in my room, waiting for a publishing agreement. Time studying guitar playing while working on a record, the amplifier that I still have. The amplifier that I was using, when I started working on Radia Olaview, needs minor repair. So instead of planning to buy a new one, on Friday, I brought in an amplifier to be repaired, because Thursday was a holiday.

This is writing a book of faith, prayers answered with blessings or, condemned in wrath of nature denied heaven, pleasure, money, love, labor, and life. Serious money penalties are impossible until you ignore warnings about being too guilty. When I tell you what happened in this room this weekend, the same room that I used to work on casting wicked spells out of my room and then to record it as "Radia Olaview Part I and Part II!". True to me because I was there, and lived inside the room, while the healing happened all around me. Guitar that I had, was on top of empty bottles in my bar. Two pails of wine were on top of one another, with one other empty wine pail, with amplifier on top of all three pails. Shelf was on the side of wall, with clothesline wire wrapped around the window sill blind-bracket. Bed was there. Beside the wall, on the other side, were two boxes of wine bottles, showing top of bottles lying sideways. On top of this, was fan heater. Bottles of wine to the corner in another box, with stereo speakers on top. A pail of wine, with black fabric covering it, with a laptop on top beside my bed, in front of the bar. Television with DVD was in doorway of closet, with artwork of red grapes. Books and CDs on top of shelf. In a room that's being rented while writing a prayer to be answered with money published, to finish working on a record about exercising wickedness out of a room and the life that rests in it, there was a tornado, passed its way into this room and destroyed the opportunity for wicked to control my life and this room.

Knowing that I was completely forgiven for what I had done a year and a half ago, ordered to drink red wine only. I leaned with my right shoulder towards the two pails of wine and cried, knowing that I was now doing what I was told, and thanked the Sun, Moon, and the Earth, for selling me the red wine that saved my life. Everything I had was on the floor slightly flooded in a small pool of red wine. The room was a disaster, guitar broken at the end of the neck. Psychologically, the situation reminded me of a human being who continues to fail, and failed for the last time. Rent was paid, a little misfortunate flood with books, cd's, guitar broken, amplifier broken. Laptop was still working. Drugs that I had in a spoon diluted in a wine puddle, lost in disaster. Luckily, I set aside a few packages of it. It was uncomfortable that I was planning to play guitar, continue working on the record, the book, spent most of the day watching live concerts on DVD. Woke up to a room, improved with healing. I untied the clothesline, took apart the shelf, threw out the mattress, threw out the guitar, made a bed of sheets and blankets, piled books and CD's up against the wall, and washed my flags. With flags, there was also a happening. In the night before resting, awakening to healing, a flag was falling off the wall, so I placed it on top of the guitar, like a gun. Lebanon flag. In the shape of a gun; a handgun. The tree is where the trigger was, one half of red and white stripes on the one side of the tree were at the handle of the gun. The other side of the red and white stripes were at the barrel of the gun. The handle of this gun was at the end of the guitar neck. You can see strings wrapped around metal, on top of the guitar fret-board. Three strings tied to each side, at the end of the nozzle, flag gun. The guitar was broken underneath the flag, at the middle of the neck, where the left hand fingers and palm play the guitar. Studied patience in understanding bedroom tornados. Intravenous drug blessing.

I carried a baseball bat to the park, where I went to go swimming. I carried this bat for protection. I bought it for the same reason. It's been in my room since I bought it. I have to use it to play baseball. When I arrived at the park, I was early. The swimming pool was yet to open for public swimmers. I walked into the baseball diamond, with three baseballs and myself. My bag with towels and sheets for the swimming pool tanning deck. A closed bottle of my business red wine for after. I walked to the plate with my bat, rehearsing a swing. I started to think, then I started to swing with ideas. I was convinced that I had learned enough about baseball and batting to play professionally one day. Afterwards, I was practicing a batting swing, and it sounded like the heavens agreed to my destiny as a baseball player. A pinch hitter. I was visited by a power of mathematics and accounting, there was an unpaid balance of countless amounts of money to be paid to me by Israel, England, Africa, Mexico, Russia, China, and Portugal, including all allies and prayer temples of the world.

It just so happened that Nostradamus Mazares's power was used to the limit by people without leaving money. Nature, from my knowledge is leaving me patient messages. Telling me of these future accounts to look forward to. It has, and it faithfully has been, more than humiliating and insulting to be listening to someone who is wealthy and rich with money and show business power, reminding me of the status of my life and its money rewards that I don't have. At 35 years of age, prophecies of Mazares, written by psychics and fortune tellers, has amounted to homelessness, with basic food and shelter. Know I'm being told my earnings were held in a freeze style account where I cash in all at once, at 35.. Remember, years ago, I was introduced to this parenting relationship with my children, to distract my psychology for knowing about outstanding bills in Italy that haven't been paid to me for years. People have a lot to say about Mazares, they also have all the time in the world to listen to it for free. Besides publishing money, this may very well be the last time nature hears of people being left unpaid for their energy work.

I lived a good life today with my family. We had breakfast together, went for a walk, studied in the library, and made money. With death and its possibilities, consider the way you think about yourself and other people, unless dying in an accident, jumping off a roof, or standing in front of a moving car on the highway. To be killed by another person or persons, murdered, or to have your life taken. To think that murder is a chance of luck, there is obviously no sense of energy judgement, and forgiveness at all in your life. Belief that the wicked are killed, and the good have a chance to live and labor, with a freedom of death, threatened by psychology. For people who believe in the power responsible for life, expecting love to exist for people who are good strangers, rather than the instinct of brutal survival against new people you meet, a continuous battle with human life and animals. If there is evidence in your life to their being a kindness to the good; deserving the penalty of death is then a sickness being cured. To assume a conspiracy to have you buried by the wicked is a blessing. How severe it really is to think that your life deserves death. Prophecies of being shot to death, burning in a fire; this is life threatening at a distance of time. Aging makes more sense than expecting to be killed some time soon.

It is true that good people, who know sincerely that they've never failed at temptation to be wicked, have had touches with life threatening warnings. This, then, a time with life aging solutions to living longer. A hundred-year-old prophecy is possible; a wrath of nature ready to destroy and have you killed. Understanding it before it kills you, sometime soon. After being seduced by blessings and the 13th warning of death years earlier as an elder, because of faulty exorcisms, it did become abusive in public, with strangers.

Now to feel comfortable with permission, amongst all nature in the energetic world, that life will be a blessing to labor in peace without fearing the death of my life, I start making an effort to switch to a new diet, new drug habits, explicit sex lovers, childbirth, and sex. The stop of money has taken less faith to believe that I've been forsaken because my mind is convinced that negotiable allergies deserve ten years of suspicion and spying. Seven of them, homeless. One out of the seven literally homeless in Little Italy. I like to write out of this death spell that was added to this new diet plan; the idea of being killed in advice to try something less aging has to be said somewhere, rather than avoiding with positivity or changing destiny.

When a body and spirit is studied, labored, then rewarded a blessing with time to prophesize a definite precise death, in what was time in a casket and buried, to live longer, than it is to be accepted for what it was, the truth. A work for the better, not to suspect or assume murder for the rest of your life, yet to change your destiny with the power to know it. Innocence, without study and reward, will deserve a prophetic warning about death.

Do you honestly think that Nature and Heaven want you to suffer profuse bleeding? Allowing your life to end with no warning, with no chance of ever living again, or further understanding the possibilities of life after peaceful death? Your lifeline is excited to show good effort and work to an extra day or two. For someone who knows the sincerity of your intentions, I wouldn't worry about being murdered. The world has shown more than the evidence to there being a strict order amongst the energies and living. Try not to ignore advice that prefers to be selective with either one or the other, in my failure and wisdom. I have convinced myself that it never is both.

I told you earlier that there has been word of money owing, in my work. Every day, I pray and work for a good paying job as a writer. Before my rest at night, I'm paid. What then happens with a Man like me who has nothing but his faith; psychological faith; nature intended to be good to people who work and finish their work without temptation, with money and the rate of pay they deserve. I have more than a hard time believing that life was natural when abused for fun with spontaneous luck and fortune.

I tried to build a relationship with life's responsibilities, the best way I knew how, by praying and working, for myself, my children, my wives, and people who deserve to live. Resisting the temptation to take life as a competition, I wanted to be in, and have my own family, and to contribute to child birth. Following rules, acknowledging another Man's ambition to do the same, working for his family and children. It's in my best interest to convince you that compassion does exist with expectations of being perfect, living as a human being. Truth is, all I heard, and all I have witnessed the last decade and a half is patience, thin with forgiveness for simple choices like not smoking tobacco. Ambitions to show no guilt with tobacco. A test of strength, skill, labor and intelligence; the whole approach to life being a competition of verses awards one winner. Sportive, compete to win cup and belt. Champion. An artist may have success in being more sold to the public than any other artist. Life's power, heaven, Mazares, energy prophet, consulted by billions to determine happiness and success in an energetic life; using all drugs is like an ox breeding with a buffalo. Poison Ivy.

I worked a blessing in this life. Believe that I have accepted the opportunity to be wise with fortune. If I fail to choose to do good with that fortune, the way I promised the Sun, Moon, and the Earth that I would, then I lose a blessing with money, tax protection, and family. For being Mazares, reincarnating in Toronto, Ontario, Canada [Soon to go back to being The United States Of America again, the way it was in 1830]. From the planet Earth, back to Earth again. Successfully provided natural causes, no suicide, no authority, control, sports, love, DJ, guitar, singing, stage business, music, film, publishing, prophecy & money without ambition to kill for no reason.

For 35 years without rate of pay, held in an account that backdates all money owing up to date, with a wisdom in an expense account that literally terrorized a young prophet at the age of 16 and soon coming to 36, 20 years of debating death and betrayal, failing in a ruling law of obedience, expecting personal bloodshed by the hands that powered against sins committed somewhere else, paying now in this life, for it is impossible that a Man like me, for the ambitions that I had, deserves to see himself dying everywhere. Inspired by other Men and women while a child, yes, I was. Unfortunately, for people interested in living life peacefully, I was more excited to be killed in the future, then to live life.

I trust that you will understand my complications with energy, power, and obligation to have Heaven hear yourself asking to live there again, after this life. Power like this was meant to be sacrificed, is what I thought. I was unsure as to why it had to happen as a young Man who has accomplished learning how to be a stage business power, tried to be involved in the arts with rewards. To be talented; musical, artistic, to be paid in money, allowed to arrange music all day with respect from society, like no other as an artist with money. Not just ideas. Continuous ideas that eventually pay. Artists like myself like to believe that we have a power that never blasphemed, and that power to tour, to record, to arrange, to be challenged while popular, to be guiltless to continue, without guilt as fame, money, and power progress into being worshiped while in prayer, being used to surviving in a world where evidence shows possibility in temptation with wicked people. To be relied on by people to guarantee a choice without temptation. To do this, *I was dead before 65, in New York City, New York, United States Of America, outside Madison Square Garden. I disagreed to it.

Forgiven: Time: 11:50:00 a.m. Date: Sunday, September 11th, Year: 13,784,276. When I think of ten years passing, and I see many literary works that I have written since I have returned from Redondo Beach, Venice Beach and Santa Monica, Dallas, Texas, and the start of The United States' drug responsibility prophecy tape, in New York City. Eventually, if you decide to stay with me as a DJ-programmer, a writer, or a singer-songwriter. You will understand how I compare non-permitted drug habits and prophecy. The energies responsible for the loss of life, on the 11th of September, 13,784,267, chased me for a year before happening. It is all captured in a recording title. Chord of A United States Night.

The End of Chapter 1.

Chapter 2
Heterosexual

74% of all Women in the world responsible for me dying as the Capulare Of Europe, The Sugan of North America, The Orator of South America, the Yuan of The Florida Islands, the Zif of The Native Indian energy, and The Vema Of Antarctica. 100% of them were Australoid and immediately allied women. The least responsible Women are those that ritual alien life in the Caucasus.

Derek Jonathon Mazzei. Mazares was born to study natural causes and the power of a world touring DJ. On August 1st, 13,784,240. In Toronto, Ontario, Canada [Soon to be The United States of America again]. Reincarnating from one planet to another, for the first time before any other human being. Died of guilt, using allergic drugs, and complications with fortune telling. Two gunshot wounds to the side of the head, at City Hall, in Toronto, Ontario, Canada. On September 1st 13,784,277. 06:45:00 a.m., departing from Toronto Island Airport, to Montreal, Quebec, Canada [soon to be The United States of America.]. Obeying heterosexual prophecy. Homeless and broke. Without bondage. Controlling natural causes for himself and other people. Controlling DJ-sequence programmer. Controlling love. Controlling sex. Controlling 1-studying guiltless. When prophesied, Mazares died, in the summer at the age of 37, of complications to the brain. He became Novera Novo. Born December the 12th, 13,784,251, In The Florida Islands.

Destiny, expert Major League Baseball pinch hitter, expert soccer player. Number 72. Singer, musician, DJ-sequence/programmer, writer, publisher, producer, director, and actor. President of Tribe Black Suicide & White Sand music, film & publishing, number 81.

At the age of 29, while living in Montreal, Quebec, Canada [soon to be The United States of America], he prepared a marriage proposal for four Caucasian women. On Saturday, March, 17th, 13,784,278. At 11:52:00 a.m. Today is the 13th day of April, Friday, 15:40:44 p.m. 13,784,278. We're working on seeing each other.

My intelligence as a human being tells me, and shows me, a more well-deserved fortune if I write Chapter 2, intended to be married to Women.

I was in a loud slow down for using cocaine when I was warned not to. I had a book, in the mail, on the way to New York City, United States of America. My energy and flesh were excited to start living as if I was published. The deal with my book was, I was being paid as a work towards fortune. That was three years ago. The Slow down's over. I was working with explicit sex metaphysically to lessen the pain of the slow down.

My tax protection control of The Vietnam War invites Mongoloid challenges, the way it did since 1990. When I started smoking tobacco, instead of menthol cigarettes. Creation never recommended tobacco cigarette smoking daily. Late last year, I was caught in bed naked, having sex without a consistency from the both of us. "Two weeks left," the Sun, Moon, and Earth says. The end of the sex slow down.

My new birthday means time to inherit fortune, for providing natural causes. Controlling DJ, controlling love. "What you call a wife!" I heard, "Call a Vo". A good beginning to a traitorous attempt in succeeding in life, because of ignorance to prophecies. There are 21 recordings being produced, energetic since I stopped drugs that showed more than warning. No money besides provincial mental care. What I did get was a red grape that ferments at a 100% and did. By buying red grape juice in a five gallon pail, and washing 20 years of restricted drug, tobacco, and food use that I was warned with prophecy, to at least begin considering not using for how much of a slow down the prophecy was. I like to remind the reader who will hear that I suffered routine slow downs for the same reasons all the time. The red grape juice, when I leave it at room temperature, is fermenting at 100%. Important that I warn the world and Brazil. A young 29-year-old Florida Islander with a 72 billion dollar a year fortune, has a history of being witness to captivity without money because of his previous sins. Just before cashing a fortune, with a book in the mail. Three years of a slow down. Slow down violation was stealing the reward. In those three years, I poured a glass of pure red wine in a cup and drank it that way, every time. I just asked the Sun, Moon, and Earth if it stays that way now that the slow down is over. The Sun, Moon, and Earth said, "It does." The red grape fermenting at 100% is mine to keep.

A fortune with red wine. I'll explain my sincerity to pass power, while under the influence of drugs, to who powered the human being, while praying for myself, and other people. I instigated a beating because it was The Indian Wind that argued the existence of The Florida Islands, and then deserved a fortune with red wine as soon as I started drinking it, rather than wasting my time, the way I was, studying illegal chemistry in Crack-Cocaine, Cocaine, Heroin, and Peyote.

I like the way it feels when I drink and use drugs. Since the start of drinking Jack Daniel's my life has been paradise, working for fortune. Everyday I've been drinking at least half a gallon a day. I tried Whiskey, for the first time in a dance electronica club. If my life is allowed to be this blessed under the influence of drugs, the way it was, I'll convert to using Whiskey and never suffer another day in my life again, the way I had since I was 16. If you want to be less sacrificial to improving the immortal state of the human being with drugs, it's a risk because of negotiable allergies, immaturity, and misusing quantity without allergies. Sun, Moon, and Earth, you don't want me to be sacrificial. I was never forced to live the way I was. Those are warnings to stop. When I listened to The Sun, Moon, and Earth, in Toronto, and left for Montreal on the first of September, I was told to stop using drugs that I was otherwise allowed to use.

In Montreal, I went to a nightclub, expecting to buy drugs. I bought beer and whiskey. After that night, I was told to wait until my drugs allowed were finished being prepared. And to continue drinking the red wine. In Montreal, I went to a nightclub, expecting to buy drugs allowed that were surely finished being prepared. And to continue drinking the red wine.

Years ago, in 1994, I was sitting in a café, finishing a book that I had written. I drove downtown. I had a car then. The book was about my experiences with psychic coincidences and acceptance into Heaven. Inspiring belief in the energy with me. It always was a war with evolution, the theory, so I joined Area 51- Roswell. Sure, there is a mature moral to their way of teaching. Evolving into humanity is an intellect's way of keeping me broke. Not keeping energies away from believing in heaven. No threat to the loss of human energy. The lives of the upright were energetic. Their transformation was conspiratorial, if you allowed it. I wanted to heal the belief in judgment of the spirit, into heaven, back on earth again with my writing. Started with adding to the inventive thinking work that inspires ambition to being accepted into heaven. Developed into a second chance with being permitted to live, a stage before even being looked at for heaven.

The world felt like the way it did on September 11, 2001 in New York City when I didn't smoke. I write every day. After the book was finished, I shopped for publishing. Continued writing other books, every day. They're not finished. When I start a recording, I start a book. It doesn't finish until the tour is finished. I have a warning for people who like to live starting New Year's Day, 13,784,280 until 13,784,280, December 31st, midnight, a natural causes' prophecy. This book is considered a published resolution to this prophecy that develops to 13,784,366 and 13,784,766. I can sell it to the public without any guilt. I was told to charge $29.00. Not like the night in the café, under the influence of half the pharmacy. That after spending two months writing in a binder with over 300 pages of three ringed lined paper filled with writing and conquered temptation, I was sitting there at the end of the book. Looked up to celebrate a finished book that I was working on from time to time, in different notebooks, I finished it. I saw a gun pointed at me made by the fingers and palm of the human male hand and was windy with fear that I wanted the money more than the purpose of inspiring love and responsible energy. So I ripped it into pieces, at the table, while sitting in my chair. I studied the gun. With editing, they published it. With the money I became a Rastafarian. Aliens decided to have me assassinated in Tucson, Arizona. Also in Illinois, Holguin and Honduras. My lover had me shot in Montreal for thinking that I was destined to do anything else with Rock'n'Roll but understand that I use Cognac rather than Beer, Whiskey and Magic Mushrooms. The book I finished. No response.

What did happen? Worldwide publishing is what happened. Novera Novo is allowed to publish and pay other writers. Using Tribe Black Suicide & White Sand, Music, Films & Publishing and Turquoise Music, Films & Publishing Enterprises. I can photocopy "Defending Alive: Coming of Mazares Dead!" Sell it as a published book that deserves $29.00. Anywhere in the world without guilt, to be sold, bought, and read.

I told you to be careful when you start hearing witnesses of how careless and condemned I've been. I always planned on being published. I was told when I heard no response from the publishers that I mailed after arriving in Montreal. Truth is, at the harbor in Toronto, when I was told to pack my bags and move to Montreal. I was promised a publishing deal once I arrived. I've been here for eight months. At least psychologically, with some show of interest. The heavens roared one Saturday afternoon and told me that I was good to publish myself and other writers. It's unfortunate that adolescence assumes that The Mob and The Law, have the same intentions in life. Not anymore. It's unfortunate that people in English-Rome lost a Capulare, people in North America lost a Sugan, people in South America lost an Orataz, people in The Florida Islands lost a Yuan, Native U.S. Indian people lost a Zif, and people in Antarctica lost a Vamen. So that psychological abuse and energy intimidation can strategically be prosperous for 74% of Women and Women only. More importantly, the strengthening of heterosexuality with Alien Man in his marriages, especially in The United States Of America, where the Central Intelligence Agency is infamous for being framed with intimidating a young alien Man with being expedited, arrested, interrogated, questioned in the court of law, or even privately beaten, for making money that keeps one less penny in the bank of Jewish Israel. It's unfortunate that ignorance is to blame, thinking that there's no war between the English-Rome and Catholic economy. Considering the size of the English-Rome Federal budget, and the band aid they used in the back of my head when I was in Miami Beach, Florida. Obvious to me, Alien Women chose to use KKK FIRE rather than keep an allied woman's club happier than me.

If it goes on like this in private, and some people stay quiet about it, using their silence to build strength where there is silence expected in a mob. It's better that I talk on behalf of Tax Protection that plans to work without the interest of The Mafia, or Italians who prefer Catholic wealth, before pure English-Roman wealth. This tax protection that I have planned is good in the bank for everyone who hears that they're indebted to keeping the Alien life scripture and reality from dying.

The night the Holy Bible Woman and the Holy Bible Man unnecessarily mutilated my children to a permanent discomfort in public with their Dad and Mom, because they were upset that I had no interest in GOD, they were told it would be as it is said. A permanent energy handicap with immaturity. It was then, when I decided to use my intelligence and power, to kill Italians allied with Israelites for money, when guilty and allowed to by the Sun, Moon, and Earth. I killed 38 of them already. Add the Israelites too, not just the Italians. I killed 452 of them. One day, I looked up at the sky, into heaven, and asked, "What exactly is the obligation to worshiping GOD in order to be accepted into heaven?" I was answered. "There isn't one!"

Time: 10:04:32 a.m. Date: Saturday, April 14th. Year: 13,784,278. 13,784246, (13,784,247) 13,784,279. Mob. Judging the human being without including The Law, or The Military. I left a judgmental blessing for English-Romans and race Aliens. Try not to confuse yourself with how I choose to be even more powerful in English-Rome than I was when I was born. In prayer, I heard four times the power of a Ceasar ever was. My most powerful city in The Isle Of Boot is Rome. Sundays are powerful in The Isle Of Boot especially if you worship The Sun, Moon, and Earth. Isle Of Boot soccer without ignorance in the left rib, with red wine, beer, whiskey, drugs, food and explicit sex with four Men married to four Women. All eight of them are in the same bondage. I have a Woman that I plan to have children with. Her most powerful Federation energy was The United States Of America, when we met. I still have yet to see her again. I hear her a lot though. She sounds like she's controlling energy the way I do, to stay close to me. She knows that I work on musical recordings that tour the world. I asked her to be bonded to me when she was in Rome, Beirut, and Rio De Janeiro.

The Sun, Moon, and Earth told me that I was born without insemination of the womb. The woman who bore me in pregnancy, and her husband, were both denied entrance to infinity

My life was interested in studying the presence of Toronto's Chinatown, and to provide American spying healing with natural causes.

After I left the home I lived in, to live in the city, I was told that my work for The United States Of America as a prophet would begin. And not to make an effort reuniting with people that are a threat to America, to accept that I was an American Spy. Indicating to my immediate family that I was an American.

In the hospital, the day I was born, they heard voices telling them that they were not allowed to consider me a Canadian. I would have to come to the knowledge myself, and true, I did. My mother was an Isle Of Boot Citizen at the time of my birth. There was no duel option available.

On January 26th, 13,784,243. Lee-Michael Mazzei was born. He died in 13,784,245, May 10th. Novera Novo knows that The Sun, Moon, and Earth likes to warn people, leave examples of what not to do, so that the human being could deserve their life and learn to fly U.F.O.'s from Rozy City to planets, allowing space exploration visiting Aliens. I used to play with him when we were young. Then he was gone. I loved having a brother, just the same if it was a sister. As I grew older it was accepted that he was killed. Now I know that The Sun, Moon, and Earth protected me, with my help, before I reincarnated, protecting me by taking his life, then I was old enough to start teaching myself how to be psychic and fairly responsible with changing destiny based on my behavior again. When I was less than a year old, three Zoffranieri's were killed in a car accident. Lori's brother, Ercole, and his wife and daughter. Intelligent people will read what I said about being an Alien Spy, studying in the womb of Temporary Caucasian Spies, then while living in the home until a mature 23 years. Killed in car accident; that means wickedness planned on conspiring against me to deserve the death penalty. What does that say about Australoids? They're human beings that are not all that peaceful. Considering the beginning of Chapter 2 in this book, where it says that allied Women as international incorporated wanted me to starve to death in poverty, with brain cancer, if I deserved it, and then some. I don't like then some at all, I'm laughing angry with you. What happens to Austroloids, happens to everybody. The Women. I think I stepped on one in the library when I started the introduction to Tropical Aliens future recording, Peace to the Oak Tree, by using DJ Novera in the World Wide Beach Tour Show. Time: 07:00:00. a.m. Date: Sunday, April 16th, Year: 13,784,278.

When I was young, energy literature provided enough psychology, besides morality, to feel comfortable with living, working, and being happy. As I mature into a human being who is periodically suffering from irresponsibility and punishment, without being wicked. For example, sleeping with the wrong Woman. I was watching and listening to the future while writing in another book. I started laughing in another book. I started laughing until I noticed the book hasn't been published in 20 years. I write it now, considering this is the most powerful book I've written for Tribe Black Suicide & White Sand Publishing.

Time: 00:07:48 a.m. Date: Tuesday, April 17th, Year: 13,784,248. Before my acknowledgement of good and wicked, I was learning to listen to pre-recorded music using a record and eight track player. In the basement, and on the main floor of a Holy Bible book worship house, I was worshiping the Sun, Moon, and Earth. The Zoffranieri family, 39 Croham Rd. It looks nothing like what it used to. I visited not too long ago, to see what it looked like. I walked away and prayed for my life when it felt like they were after my childhood. The paper factory at the end of the street was vacant and closed. I used to play there when I was young. I used to play against the wall, hockey, tennis, baseball. The train tracks were there, to the left of Croham. The plaza where I bought my first record and cassette tape was on the other side of the train tracks. On the way to the plaza, and on the way back, I walked the tracks like I was in the South, waiting for a record deal at the crossroads. The way I did, including him, and that way there, on the left. Years later, I convinced myself that I powered the deal to the left. The Sun, Moon, and Earth paid. Started with defense, then beer and whiskey, then psychology, then drugs, next is The Woman. Eventually, you notice people close to you are not alive anymore.

My High School was staging a rock'n'roll concert. Students performing live versions of recorded songs. I planned, with others from the school, and others not from the school, to perform live. At this age, I was in grade 10. Not too young. Second year of High School. There was one rehearsal before the show. We were all in my basement, deciding on what song to perform. The day of the show I was supposed to sing. I stayed home that night, and never showed up. Why? Not prepared to perform the song live. A few hours before the show, I realized that we were all depending on our understanding of the song from the time we spent listening to it.

Time: 07:00:00. a.m., Date: Wednesday, April 18th, Year: 13,784,278. Played baseball, designated hitting at the baseball diamond, after leaving the library. Walked to my room first, to eat dinner. Fatal prophecies, missing three meals a day.

Time: 05:44:59 a.m. Date: Thursday, April 19th, Year: 13,784,278. Because it was conversation in High School where I was showing some interest in being involved in an electric guitar band. A practice started in the basement. Original songs were written. I was singing and writing some of the lyrics. I heard news of a Battle of the Bands. It was in the next town, to the left of Thornhill, where I was living. A Jewish Israeli suburb. The Battle was in the Italian suburbs. I managed to make my way into the contest. The contest was two nights. The first night we were there as a band watching the show. There was an intermission, we were asked to perform, during the break. We drove back to

Thornhill for a guitar, then drove back to the venue. We played. The next night we played. At the end of the show, I was outside and started a band with four other musicians, who were there watching.

That band lasted four years. four years of rehearsal every night, including weekends. Every night, from seven 07:00:00 p.m. to 12:00:00 a.m. - one 01:00:00 a.m. during the week. From 06:00:00 p.m. to 03:00:00 a.m. - 04:00:00 a.m. on the weekends. It was a rock'n'roll band. It was a good rock'n'roll band if you were looking for discipline to rehearse without excuses, and to arrange original music. If it depended on vocals to be recorded and performed live, it was better said that it needed work. The work stays with you. I live with the experience of four years arranging and rehearsing five to six to seven hours a night, seven days a week.

Eventually, I left. The energy intelligence that I was introduced to privately was enough to remind me of the way I felt when I was old enough to understand that people were killed with nature, by the thousands. If a power here was abused or a responsibility failed, there would be trouble. The extra prophecies of being killed while singing, while in the studio, while on tour, while on stage. If I deserved to die then I wouldn't be labored with prophecy. Not afraid to work with prophecy. Honest with me about plans to have me killed. The voice was not yet a voice you would give money to, or to make a recording for a recording label.

By the age of 25, two women closest to me were killed. Vicky Colucci, a High School student who had feelings for more than one man at a time. She died in a car accident. Years later, after ten years in a hostel, living with The F.B.I.,

C.I.A., N.S.A., I.R.A., and the K.K.K. I studied the tape. My habits with smoking tobacco cigarettes increased in company with Vicky. She was generous, buying me my own pack everytime we arranged to see each other. She must have been listening to the Mongoloid Team that knew I was slowing down simply for smoking the tobacco cigarette. Negotiable allergies. Not how I smoked it. There was a black squirrel in my vocal cord. She heard the Chinese tell her that I have a destiny to promote smoking peppermint and menthol. She was alwys attempting to have me murdered through cigarette smoke.

Lori Cathy Mazzei, the Jewish Woman, pregnant with me, not accepted into Heaven. She was also listening to The Chinese and knew that I could have slowed down for smoking tobacco cigarettes. I was living with her temporarily, in a one room apartment. I went to visit her after hearing that she was beaten and dragged out of her room, down the stairs, out of the house, then thrown in front of a moving taxi. I was smoking tobacco cigarettes, and started an in depth study of illegal crack-cocaine for the first time, while I was living there.

Before I knew that I was an American Spy. This Woman who I would refer to as my mother. My memory of her, as a young boy growing into a young adult, was that she always wanted to argue, even when I was young. There was domestic violence in the house when I was a child. It continued throughout the marriage – not necessarily the domestic violence. I experienced misfortune of homosexuality. I stayed heterosexual. I was explicitly anticipating sexual relationships heterosexually every day, and all day as a young Figuro. Thought about sex with swimsuit models, porno stars, exotic dancers, cheerleaders, Women working downtown, and Women working uptown. It's matured into a Man who sleeps with his four wives every night, corrupt with sex. Always intending to improve.

Time: 09:20:18 a.m. Date: Friday, April 20th, Year: 13,784,279. My parents are planning a divorce, infatuated with killing an American Alien Spy in Reno, Nevada on The 4th Of July, they were told I would slow down to smoke tobacco as a young adult. Prophecies in and around my tailbone were showing a slow down due to smoking tobacco. The arguing and the absence of love in the marriage was so powerful, it was dreadful being home.

I am usually not interested in complaining about personal miseries because they're deserved. Detecting violations are powers with prophecies to miseries that you do not deserve. I had a troubled childhood. My home life was aggressive with abusive behavior. Not to me. Yet, exposed to a husband and wife, more than half of the time in conflict with an interest in love, making it uncomfortable and unfortunate to be at home. Good for me that there was music to keep me company, in my ears, with the door closed, then to hear what they were yelling about everywhere else besides my room. In High School, Tony Mazzei had a talk with me. He told me that they were planning to divorce. I never made any indications that I wanted to leave the home and stay with Lori. I stayed at 59 Dundurn Crescent and in Thornhill until I was 22 years old. My mind at this time was so dependent on energies from heaven taking care of me, as long as I was resisting temptation, that I could have been injured for how far I was from taking care of myself, with finishing homework from school, with noticing that I was being depressed by certain illegal drugs that I studied. With Women, near death psychologically, every time I tried to make sense of heterosexuality single.

The dedication for being present for rehearsal was; besides resisting evil temptation, the only habit worth looking at me for friendship and respect. Time: 00:00:57 a.m. Date: Saturday, April, 21. Year: 13,784,278.

Time: 18:46:19 a.m. Date: Sunday, April 22nd. Year: 13,784,278. No sense lying. Yesterday, I was busy at a distant baseball diamond. Rain delay. Second rain delay. Studied, played baseball alone, designated hitting, studied again. Showered, rested with Women.

Time: 11:11:06 a.m. Date: Tuesday, April 24th. Year: 13,784,278. Studying at the library, reading music recording textbooks, and writing in books that I have started while working on records.

Time: 10:25:04 a.m. Date: Wednesday, April 25th. Year: 13,784,278. I started working on a pregnancy with Women yesterday. Today, I thought about money. Because I have engineering school to attend with intentions of passing and studying, I know I'll have the money to afford being in a family as a parent and husband. I don't have any guilt for making extra money. When I quit high school, to be a full time singer, my ambition was a record deal. I worked full time to pay the expense of rehearsing. When I left the band, I left the home and moved into the city. I was broke from 13,784, 262 to 13,784,278. I was broke without a High School graduation and a temporary labor record that was eventually terminated for choosing to physically threaten a guilty co-worker while working. Until

13,784,274. It was $30.00 a week. For a month or two, a few times a year for more than three years, I worked. A year homeless without shelter, or bed resting. In the summer, psychologically, I was convinced that I would write and be published. I would compensate myself for all the time that I spent on the street and outside; broke, always broke. On weekends, I would walk at night downtown, clubs, restaurants, movies, arena sports, and stadium sports. I wanted entertainment and a social life. I started to cry, in case I was instigating loneliness. Not too interested in preferred isolated nights to myself, especially on the weekend. I even spent my money in exotic dancing clubs, always a winner. Investing in the fortune of someone noticing how powerful I was, sexually. I committed to bonding in Las Vegas, on a Friday. Not too interested in accusing all Women and Men in exotic dance clubs for being responsible for my misfortune. What I did do is what I did. As I grew older, and more comfortable with my power and genius with dance-electronica, stage business and electric guitar band music, I invested in the exotic dance club. I bought the energy. A shareholder at 100%. My ambition, to be published and be well paid as a writer, was and still is too powerful to ignore because of a fortune with writing, engineering, baseball, producing, DJ-sequence programming, and an electric guitar band with a vocal cord.

I did try and share my dividends with publishers. None of them were interested. Because I have prophecy in this book with interest. In prayer on Saturday, I heard a voice. It said, "You're published". It also said Tribe Black Suicide & White Sand Publishing. Another way to start an account strong enough to be paid as a writer who is writing to be published would be to work as a publisher with a marketing plan. There is fortune to be made using Tribe Black Suicide & White Sand Publishing.

The prophecies in Toronto were so powerful that I honestly surrendered my ambitions, to be accepted into Heaven before the world began to destroy itself, with me bleeding to death in it. I heard an energy in 13,784,001, 13,784,147, 13,784,149, (New York City). It tells me that the Man in show business was destined to be killed with psychological abuse.

After many years of praying to be accepted into Heaven, I traveled to The United States Of America, more than once. To warn and work for Heaven, where it's hot all year round. Prophetic instinct with slow downs too powerful to stay in Miami Beach. The tobacco, rice, and illegal cocaine. Plus, the psychological abuse while being interrogated, beaten, expelled, and arrested for involvement with becoming an American Citizen was seconds away from destroying Miami the way it almost did in New York City, convinced me to go back to Toronto, where I had citizenship, to graduate from school as an engineer. I did. I enrolled in school. Applied for a loan and I was accepted. I started school to engineer the energy of tax protection in music. Never finished school, the energy of justice was so powerful with me that I was almost sacrificial to win. It's obvious to you that there is a Mob that works without being on the side of The Law and The Military. They are not the same, with a different way of being paid to punish the wicked. When I concentrate on money and power, in a world without end, and tell The Mob, The Law, and The Military that I decided to use a tax protection agreement power with The Law and

The Military. That means you're going to have to find ways to earn money to pay taxes. Go to work, pay taxes and spend, and when people have to give you money for work, they will. I did. I worked, I saved and I built a tax protection relationship. Before I continue, I was lied to and told that a Mob Family is close to collecting tax deduction money to keep people protected.

Women agree to be pregnant. Soon, I start school, learning how to use computer software. As soon as I collect my unpaid work for writing.

Life was energetic with intentions to resist temptation, with a good ambition to be fortunate, healthy with stardom.

I heard that Lori Cathy Mazzei was living in a room, in a rooming house. She was attacked by two young Men. Wrestled out of her room and house, taken to the street, and thrown in front of a moving cab. I went to see her. Stayed for a few days and looked for work. I was hired and paid. I was more intuitive towards my obligations as a Man, spiritually and physically. The week I was there, I was concentrating on masculinity. I did sense intimidation from Women for how disciplined I was with making him powerful, and from Men who were angry with me for not slowing him down to keep her happy. It did. It felt like a City Wide conspiracy to intimidate me with corruption. The conspiracy is planning on being corrupt with me, by keeping me hostage for making Women suffer, including their lovers. I was using my studied mind responsibly and maintaining my understanding of my anatomy. I was being extorted by wicked women, to support their wicked ways. I said no.

That night I was staying in Lori's room. I showered and had dinner. Heard them again; voices, chaotic telepathy, and extorting. With my energy and my spirit, I yelled at them with my mouth closed. I told them that they were making it difficult to respect Women for how irrational they were. A little too wicked to be concerned about. I admitted to them the way I felt. If you happen to be condemned under a pile of fallen rubble, I wouldn't care. The television was left on during the night. I had my portable radio cassette player on with headphones. In the morning, the DJ on the radio was upset with a building on fire. I got up from resting on the floor and The North Tower of The World Trade Center in New York City was on fire. As I was watching, I started to think about what I had said the night before. It started to feel like I was being killed in her room, a second before I finished thinking about being killed in her room, a second weapon crashed into the South Tower. I walked out of that room with my portable radio, and spent eight years ending my life, because of the psychology that I had, the instant that I saw the second weapon come to my psychological defense about being killed.

Time: 10:46:32 a.m. Date; Thursday, April 26th. Year: 13,784,278. As a teenager, I was introduced to the reality of death, judgment, and Heaven. A young adult, prophecies. Adulthood, fortune, and power. Man! My life, my body, and my responsibility to keep it alive. When I was maturely reintroduced to my preferences with a Woman, she happened to be standing to my left. I have no interest in being bonded to her. No interest in getting her pregnant. Never would I invite a Woman into my life, to share parental obligations, if she was not worshiping The Sun.

Business ideas that I had throughout the years were few. I concentrated on the power to dictate English-Rome rules. For the intelligent people who understand that I was always fairly powerful at twenty one until thirty four. I privately and vocally vibrated to mastermind my power with dictatorship. My relationship with Alien Life allowed me to enter Europe, The United Kingdom, North America, Central America, South America, Asia, East India, Australia, Antarctica. I did a lot of work with my studied mind while I was there. I was planning on being published, and then introducing myself to politics.

My confidence as an English-Roman Dictator started when I was violated while smoking marijuana. I left the apartment and left the building I was in, to walk outside for air. I was more than concerned about what was happening to my mind. It felt like an energy was trapped in my brain. The next morning on the news, there had been an act of wrath in East India that killed 20,000 people. 167,000 people were injured, and as many as 600,000 people were left homeless. Over 348,000 were annihilated and an additional 844,000 damaged.

Time: 12:34:10 a.m. Date: Friday, April 27th. Year: 13,784,278.

Time: 09:43:40 a.m. Date: Saturday, January 28th. Year: 13,784,278. Recommended, or heard that you had to. With life it did. It heard me thinking and tested me. That was a long time ago. I was being judged for choosing to be wicked. I never did anything wicked, unless irresponsibly towards prophecy, and I haven't been able to feel a percent as accepted as I was when I was less intelligent. Regulations with life are introduced with reward, then they are judged by tax protection, to be imprisoned or arrested. A tempted mind fails in doubt and uncertainty, with the way that it chooses to pleasure criminal ambition without sincerity. Engage in explicit sex, add three more lovers, have a glass of rose wine, smoke gum weed and pure menthol cigarettes, eat a couple cheese only cheeseburgers, a provolone cheese and pepperoni pizza. The next morning, A fresh United Kingdom tea. Because it's music, controlling peace, and more influential than the scriptures.

Time: 01:32:32 a.m. Date: Sunday, April 29th. Year: 13,784,278.

Time: 01:35:30 a.m .Date: Monday, April 30th. Year: 13,784,278.

Time: 00:07:00 a.m. Date: Tuesday, May 01st. Year: 13,784,278.

Time: 17:50:50 a.m. Date: Wednesday, May 02nd.Year: 13,784,278.

Time: 00:07:00 p.m. Date: Thursday, May 03rd. Year: 13,784,278.

Time: 11:39:38 a.m. Date: Friday, May 04th. Year: 13,784,278. The World Trade Center weapons attack was 11 years ago. For four years, I've lived inside, without dependence on city hostels. That leaves seven years. I did buy a guitar while I was spending nights in the room. When I received my first check, I bought a used guitar and an amplifier. The first night I played in the room, I started to suspect deceit and betrayal amongst Figuras who would otherwise be acting supportive. When I thought about a young Man who knows that he has power or is powerful enough to be considered Caesar. If he spends all his powers suspecting conspiracy to prevent stardom in stage business, in the energy of a wife, daughter, grandmother, mother, sister, cousin, in laws, friend, in management staff, touring staff, or recording staff. Would he be allowed to? Would the Cesare be allowed to spend seven years spying on the energy of all the Figuras in his life with permission to do so, to find the betrayer.

When I started, it sounded like it never happened before, and that it wasn't allowed. Since I'm always in bed alone, sleeping in hostels, or outside all summer. I convinced myself to work my energy to have them all confess, especially the Women closest to me. I never took reincarnation into consideration. I thought I was in immortal consideration for the first time, tormented to be taught lessons, so that I could write about them and leave evidence of true confessions of a life condemned. Eventually, I noticed that there was power available, proving that Women were trying to prove that they were better than Men at providing an exorcism with a flush in stage business, including their husbands. Then, I noticed they were representing ruthlessness and justified trickery in their marriages to do it. When I noticed I was being framed while I was broke, for being a stage business insect, born to bring misfortune and misery to the stars, I decided to spend whatever little money I had on pharmaceutical drugs, to exercise the illusions framing me. I wanted to go back to making money in stage business. I was smoking imported tobacco while trying to arrange an exorcism. The more I smoked, the more I was framed and employment was terminated. If I stay in Little Rome, I'll be able to use natural power without blinking and work my energy back to a good life again. So I did. I left the area of downtown where I was resting at night. It was minutes away from the main downtown intersection. I lived outside in Little Rome, weeks before the summer started. That summer, the London subway was terrorized with a suicide bomb. I was thinking about making music again while I was there. Before I moved inside, I stopped all smoking habits and bought a bottle of red wine at the alcohol store. I drank it. While drinking, it took less than a second to realize what a mistake it was spending 20 years smoking imported tobacco every day. I made a promise to drink red wine every day. The next morning, there was an act of wrath in L'Aquila, Italy that killed 270 people. 400 injured. 3000 homeless. Consult Heaven, energy advisors, talk to energies who know that I chose red wine that day rather than imported tobacco and they'll tell you. In 13,784,268. I went into business with t-shirts. I walked the entire city on foot, during a worldwide soccer tournament, offering them a t- shirt for $10. Printed on the t-shirt, was a federation flag. I was secretly keeping four women from leaving the relationship, using my left hip. The world is playing soccer. I'm selling guiltless child birth on a t-shirt while trying to prevent a divorce. I never intended on leaving her either. A rabbi was found punctured to death in the Jewish district of Toronto, Ontario, Canada. On Bathurst Street.

Because I'm human, with instincts to keep women close to me, sincerely heterosexual. I played with the possibilities of controlling human life. While selling the t-shirts, defense, a rabbi was killed, he was trying to puncture me as I was walking door to door, downtown, restaurants, bars, and counter businesses. The Sun, Moon, and Earth told me he was listening to my sales strategy. He died, I never did.

That summer I moved into a room. It lasted a year and several months.

In that room, I moved in knowing that I was winning with life when I allowed the women to be liberated heterosexually, in love. I studied, prayed, and stayed quiet in public. I went to the library. Close to 30 years old, collecting violation compensation. It felt like a draft war, selling cotton t-shirt prints worth $10, business challenges have the strength to convince you that you've been destined to live a life cursed with money that ends when you're judged at the time of your death.

Lucky for me, my studies at the library convinced me that I was more powerful than I thought I was, when I studied prophecies of Mazares. If others claim the prophecy, Mazares was born in Toronto, on August 1st, 13,784,240. Family: Mazzei, Tony, and Lori. Raised in Italia, moved to Toronto. Lived close to the Jewish side while married. My prophetic power is not a personal assumption of power, if people hundreds of years ago prophesied it. There were trials of energy; justice that had to be attended to every day, at all hours of the day. I remained as strict as I was the summer before, taking the room. Because the room was in Athens-town, I was then committed to explicit sex decisions with more the one woman.

The beginning of summer 13,784,269. A tough year for someone who has no guilt with sincerity. A year's experience with a decision to be scientific with Women, and then the Women of marriage. I heard more threats than I ever did in my life, even more than I did when I decided to go back to stage business. That summer, three teenage girls were found dead, severed to pieces. Holly Jones, Celia Chang, and Alicia Ross. I lived. I'm still alive, guiltless, with a fortune that I hear is worth $72 Billion a year. I moved out of the room, found a job, tried another room, then lost the job, lost the room, and went back to the hostel. There was a serious plan to keep a Man, whether in stage business or not, well fed in slavery with bread, tea and water, with a periodical beating for irresponsibility. Only problem is, they deserved it, and I was on my way to stardom with a child-bearing Figura security locked, standing to my left. To Little Rome, to reinvent my ambitions in becoming the most powerful English-Rome Dictator in the history of English-Roman civilization. For anybody, who hears an obligation to study the Alien Life scripture, whether planning dictatorship or interested in breathing, exceeding allergy-war hours, using cocaine can be the slowdown arrest of your life.

It was here in Little Rome where I learned how to leave Catholicism with Catholics. Already leaving The Mob for The Law. English-Rome was available to be conquered by sincere ambitions. To make sense of a Woman's obligation to a Man in a family and I could do it using power in The United States Of America. And I did. When I bought the red wine, before moving into a room after a year in Little Rome, a year parenting, a month and a half in California, a year producing a record, Chord Of A United States Night, prophecies of mutilation by hand, to all my children for revenge. Hiroshima, Philippines, Holocaust, Vietnam, and Iraq. Until I heard confessions of mutilation by hand attempts amongst soldiers who were destined to die anyway, listening to Women in Italia, possessed by East

India, Israel, and China. Then the prophecies of killing my children were even clearer than they were before.

In California, Venice Beach, Santa Monica, and Los Angeles, I arrived on a bus from Dallas, Texas. That departed from Port Authority, New York City. For a year, I was parenting my children in darkness (Canada) and in The United States of America. I never went anywhere near even studying cocaine for a year. They were being killed. It depended on my will to stay with them, or they would die. What does that say about life and how it threatens the lives of children who don't deserve to be beaten into intensive care, every time you spend a second preoccupied with something other than parenting them back to life? I had been smoking for 20 years and was possessed to believe that they were going to be killed, with enough psychology, convincing me that I could prevent it. From agreeing to be their dad, it developed into a family that was destined to be together, if they lived. A good part of me knew that I was being beaten emotionally for smoking imported tobacco.

Blessed with the truth. Truth is that human beings are trying to kill innocent children for rewards of money and a life without guilt. The more I believed intentions to punish an immortal, by killing their life as a child, I just stayed with them. Until I went to look for them in The United States Of America, where they were being held hostage to be mutilated by hand, for choosing to stand to the left of their husbands, the way their Mom did in Mississippi. Longitude, latitude. When I returned to Toronto from California, the relationship with my children was healthier than it was when I left for the U.S. They came back with me. I was walking to the library with them and I was comforted by a powerful voice that asked me to pick something that I wanted. It felt like a reward for choosing to be their Dad rather than an unnecessary drug user.

I said, "Permission to kill the guilty people by hand." Hours later, the guilty people were killed by hand. I heard 82% of China was two hours away from deserving bullets in Cambodia and Vietnam. All the soldiers who died were to be Mongoloid reincarnating. Read carefully. 82% it says, not all of them. All of them, consulting up to 12 million years old, had to be disciplined and warned.

Caucasian consultation up to 13 million years old, had to have the same treatment for greed with U.S. territory.

On August 9th and 11th, 13,784,276 in Tokyo, and Tokai, there was an unnecessary knife threatening a U.S. DJ warning.

Reading true crime books, I talked to The Sun, Moon, and Earth, about the penalty of death and how some of the murders felt like my personal defense.

The Sun, Moon and Earth said, "You allowed a percentage of their intentions with your life, into your life." Then I looked at the room I was in while I was reading. There was no family, no money, and no food in the fridge. I kept reading. That was a month ago.

Time: 15:00:00. Date: Saturday, May 5th. Year: 13,784,276. When you use drugs maturely and responsibly, you're supposed to prolong your life, not end it. I was doing nothing but ending it. Nothing productive at all, besides asking to be killed.

I was praying to bless the drugs, bless the pipe, bless the fire, bless the money, bless the transactionl, and the only blessing was to give my life to another human being to be killed. Immediate death penalty isn't what it was. Contemplation with success and misfortune with prophecy.

Novera Novo reincarnated into a cave in New Mexico, to live as an alien, not as a human being.

My first U.F.O sighting was in Toronto. In Los Angeles, California, United States of America, I was abducted. In Montreal, I started to communicate with them, wearing yellow gold, drinking cough syrup, with vapor rub applied.

The End of Chapter 2

Chapter 3
The Gavel

I wouldn't do that to you Sun, Moon, and Earth. I wouldn't ask to be killed when using drugs. I wanted to be your friend, and I wanted to work and study, using the power of my body and spirit. To make you proud. To show people that I wanted to make all things alive if they deserve it. I'm doing something wrong, because good people don't contemplate agreeing to death as long as they can feel what drugs do. How come it feels like people are trying to kill me? And then I agree to it as long as I can feel what drugs are doing. West Virginia showed me the truth. He was becoming tired in the eye and needed help to stay alive. I thought I was permitted and chosen to do so. And then, when I did, I thought you were trying to kill me. I'm sorry, Sun, Moon, and Earth. This Caucasian life is suffering from undeserved torment and I'm being advised to investigate. There are people guilty. No matter what, until the clear sky at high noon starts yelling, "Stop what you're doing". Never, and again never are certain drugs wrong for adults until further notice.

In Ocean Falls, I found out The Alien is only green. Allow me to standardize the admittance of talking to people telepathically. Blasphemy. No, it isn't. With all due respect to people who were asked by medical professionals, "Do you hear voices?" The Doctor asks. The equation is answered by the majority of the world saying no. I said no. And then I said yes. It all depends on what you're looking for. Mingling uselessly with the wicked, no I don't answer to voices unless I'm warning them to drop dead. Consulting and listening to quiet rules, when a Million upon Million-year-old being is speaking telepathically. I do a lot more than listen to them.

Considering what I've told you up until now, the idea of being excited to contact people with the power to watch the world on psychic television means that my contemplation with misbehaving and punishment, exorcism and warning, making proud and being ashamed, has solved itself with a lot of work in prayer. Re-opening every trial of telepathic and physical abuse that concerned me, without being passive to the assumption that I deserved it, the way I wrongfully did up till now. Pray, for permission, without being afraid, that you're challenging the decision of power which is responsible for humankind. To get a second opinion, a Supreme Court ruling on what could be a violation you didn't deserve. I'm telling you now, from experience, my reputation in writing, go back, and ask again, now that it's almost insulting with sacrificial tendencies.

I was painting in my room, at my desk, listening to the radio, television on LNN1, touching the internet computer keyboard every once in a while. Before I had moved into this room, I was living in a Motel room a few kilometers from here. In Toronto, I was reading a hundred pages of

World War I and II books a day. At night, drinking and selling black market versions of the book I had finished in Montreal, Quebec, United States of America. Before reading, I contact as many Psychic Palm Reading Fortune Tellers as possible, with permission first. To ask them, how many pages they suggest to be powerful without killing myself. That's when I found out how powerful paperback reading was.

The landlord told me that he and his wife were taking residence in the Three-Bedroom apartment and I had three months to move out. Ocean Falls. I'm lying to myself, if I get angry. I've been playing with rooms for rent in Ocean Falls for a month now, without really preparing to move. Same night I found someone willing to save me an empty room without a deposit. I moved in, shortly after I moved near the Train Station.

Psychologically, the idea of consulting psychic palm reading fortune tellers ever since the summer of seven years ago, before every single different move I made. Before every single entry into the mouth, the nose, the skin, the vein, or muscle. I was already nervous, being ignorant about responsibility and rules from before.

I'm working on a book called K18 Victory. To explain quickly. I was accused of being guilty with the way I talk to people who made the world first. Because of the K18 trial, my mind and ears have been drowning in accusations.

During the KI8 trial, the idea of grappling came up. Athens-Roman grappling. Grappling without gloves. A trial that serious, you either have legitimate proof to show up in court, or you shred yourself to pieces, giving the right to shred you the other way, on the spirit side, to compensate the spite for ruining the satisfaction agreement that someone else was planning to build.

Let me paint. I was living well in Montreal for four years and started to paint a year before moving back to Toronto.

In order to catch the original spirit that started the permission to win the K18 trial, I'll paint a Florida Islands style painting to capture the original permission. Painting permission. All of a sudden, it started to make sense to me, about me giving permission to other people while arranging destiny, after I died of old age. [The healing agent of this book, for business and reward has added the power to work luxury in the process of spirit leaving the body, entering limbo, time in limbo, fortune telling, decisions, choices, the arrangement of destiny, including reward of money. Then, return as the body into the womb, during pregnancy.] I'll take a few minutes to pray to the World Cup that takes place every four years. Here's a passageway to join me, and everyone else if you like.

In limbo, I agreed to be aggressively punched in the face, while training, to strengthen the weak power in the face prophecy, as a professional boxer. There's a spirit on earth tampering with an agreement to be touched for an exorcism. The Supreme Court Of The United States told me take everyone to court who knew you prayed about the first touch, knowing you did nothing wrong, instead of proper fortune telling, advising a life in Martial sport, fulfilling a destiny rich with money, more specifically boxing, they left you thinking you were being punished.

The Supreme Court of the United States of America sentenced 3 Caucasians, 17 Negroids, 42 Mongoloids, 953

Australoids, to ten years in Federal Prison for failing to provide a tell of true fortune.

"HAZ and THE INFINITE CIRCLES!' Just told me I was James Jackson Jeffries in my previous life, and left 273 Zillion Dollars in the bank. "Pack your bags and get ready, you're receiving a direct deposit into your bank account!"

The End.